ASIA
The Cigars of the Pharaoh
The Blue Lotus
Land of Black Gold
New Delhi
Tintin in Tibet
Cairo
Shanghai
Katmandu
CHINA
Red Sea
SAUDI ARABIA
INDIA
PACIFIC OCEAN
China Sea
n Claws
Celebes Sea
he Red Sea Sharks
Flight 714
tin in the Congo
Jakarta
INDIAN OCEAN
AUSTRALIA

TINTIN
★
LITTLE BOOK of TRAVEL

Tintin, watch out for those animals!

Tintin and Snowy
are about to discover
Chicago.

*Everyone needs to drink
and eat, especially Snowy.*

On the road again,
in the U.S.A.

One day, Snowy will put pen to paper to share his experiences.

Train-spotting has always been fun...

Snowy in ecstasy!

Maybe Tintin will become the most famous detective in the world...

Travelling is the best form of education in the world.

If you have trouble
with heights,
please
turn the page!

Snowy would rather be at home.

More fashion victims.

Spiritual enlightenment for Tintin and Snowy.

Snowy can't wait
to go home.

Yet another fashion victim.

Nobody likes looking in the mirror, early in the morning.

Drinking and diving
can be dangerous...

A flying Haddock.

We all need
to stretch our legs...

GRRRR
GRRRR

Eating should be
a pleasure
and not a danger!

Dogs don't appreciate walking on jagged rocks.

Life is full of surprises!

Let's eat!

Never drinK and climb!

As the famous song goes, "you can't always get what you want!"

There must be
an easier way
to travel.

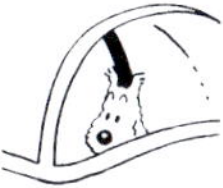

Snowy has been
waiting for this moment.

Snowy has never appreciated sitting around with a Fakir.

ISBN 978-2-87424-057-7

Printed in Belgium

Tintin in the Congo
1931

Tintin in America
1932

The Blue Lotus
1936

Tintin in America
1932

Flight 714
1968

Tintin in America
1932

King Ottokar's Sceptre
1939

Tintin and the Broken Ear
1937

Cigars of the Phara
1934

Prisoners of the Sun
1949

The Blue Lotus
1936

The Shooting Star
1942

Destination Moon
1953

Tintin in Tibet
1960

Tintin in the Congo
1931

All dates refer to the original publication in French.